W9-ABY-403

Big Bang SCIENCE EXPERIMENTS

HOT STUFF

THE SCIENCE OF HEAT AND COLD

Jay Hawkins

WINDMILL BOOKS

New York

Published in 2013 by Windmill Books, An Imprint of Rosen Publishing
29 East 21st Street, New York, NY 10010

First Edition

Editors: Joe Harris and Samantha Noonan
Illustrations: Andrew Painter
Step-by-Step Photography: Sally Henry and Trevor Cook
Science Consultant: Sean Connolly
Layout Design: Orwell Design

Picture Credits:
Cover: Shutterstock
Interiors: Shutterstock: 4–5.

Library of Congress Cataloging-in-Publication Data

Hawkins, Jay.
 Hot stuff : the science of heat and cold / by Jay Hawkins. — 1st ed.
     p. cm. — (Big bang science experiments)
 Includes index.
 ISBN 978-1-4777-0321-2 (library binding) — ISBN 978-1-4777-0363-2 (pbk.) — ISBN
978-1-4777-0364-9 (6-pack)
 1. Heat—Experiments—Juvenile literature. 2. Cold—Experiments—Juvenile literature.
 3. Heat—Transmission—Juvenile literature. I. Title.
 QC256.H39 2013
 536.078—dc23
                                          2012026223

Printed in China

CPSIA Compliance Information: Batch #AW3102WM: For Further Information contact Windmill Books, New York, New York at 1-866-478-0556
SL002559US

CONTENTS

Can you take the heat?

UP AND AWAY!

Have you ever been in a hot air balloon? They soar through the sky, carried aloft by nothing more than an envelope of warm air. This book is packed with facts and experiments exploring the incredible science of heat.

THE HEAT IS ON

What makes hot air balloons float? The air around us may not feel heavy, but it does have a weight. When it is heated, it weighs less. That's because air molecules move around faster when they're heated, and spread apart over a larger space.

GOING UP!

The burner in a hot air balloon heats the air in the envelope directly above it. The hot air is so much lighter than the air around it that it is pushed upward.

HIGHER AND HIGHER

A hot air balloon works just like a cork in water. The cork floats upward because it is lighter than the water around it, whereas the balloon floats up because it is lighter than the air around it.

MINI MELT

In this icy experiment, we will use a miniature iceberg to see how the density of water changes with temperature.

YOU WILL NEED:
- ★ Water
- ★ A small pitcher
- ★ A glass
- ★ Food coloring
- ★ $\frac{1}{3}$ cup of vegetable oil
- ★ An ice cube tray
- ★ A fridge or freezer

Step 1

Prepare some special ice cubes by adding a few drops of food coloring to some water in a pitcher.

I only seem to have green coloring. Will that do?

Step 2

Fill an ice tray with the colored water, then put it in the fridge to freeze. It should be frozen in 2 to 3 hours.

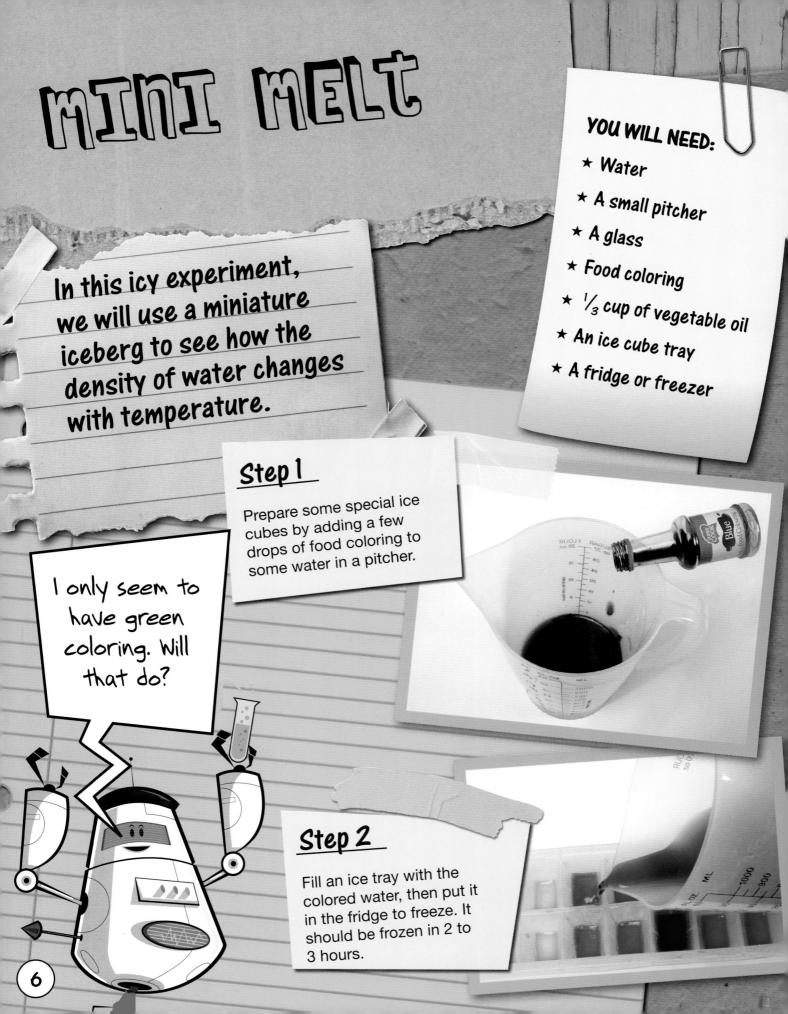

Step 3

Fill a glass ⅓ full with water.

Step 4

Pour in some vegetable oil until the glass is ⅔ full.

The water and oil form separate layers.

Step 5

Take an ice cube out of the tray and put it in the glass.

Step 6

Watch as the ice cube melts. What is happening?

Step 7

After about 30 minutes, the ice cube melts completely, the colored cold water stays at the bottom of the glass, and the oil is clear.

HOW DOES IT WORK?

When water is in its liquid form, it is denser than oil, so the oil floats on top of it. However, when the water is frozen and becomes ice, it is less dense than the oil, so the ice floats on top of the oil.

HOMEMADE SHRINK RAY

Put your mad scientist hat on as you use the power of science to shrink everyday objects!

YOU WILL NEED:

- ★ An oven
- ★ An oven mitt
- ★ A timer
- ★ Snack bags made of plastic—not foil
- ★ Dishwashing liquid
- ★ A paper towel
- ★ Aluminum foil
- ★ Brooch pins
- ★ Universal glue

Step 1

We are going to turn a full-size snack bag into a miniature one! Rinse out a bag with water and dishwashing liquid. Then ask an adult to preheat the oven to 475°F (245°C).

Monkey Snacks

BANANA

Monkey Snacks BANANA

Step 2

Dry the bag with a paper towel.

Monkey Snacks

Make sure you get rid of all the crumbs and grease.

Wrap the bag in aluminum foil.

Step 4

Fold over the ends to make an envelope.

Step 5

Ask an adult to help you place the aluminum foil envelope on the top shelf of the oven. Then close the oven door and check the temperature. Set the timer for two minutes. You need to stick to this time exactly.

We're turning trash into cool stuff with the power of heat!

Step 6

After two minutes, ask an adult to help you remove the envelope from the oven using an oven mitt. Place the envelope on a heatproof surface.

Step 7

Pat down the foil envelope with the oven mitt and then let it cool completely.

Step 8

Once it is cool, remove the shrunken bag from inside.

Step 9

Make gifts for your friends! Attach a brooch pin to the back of the miniature bags to make buttons.

You can try shrinking some other types of snack bags.

HOW DOES IT WORK?

The molecules making up the bag are in long chains called polymers, which are naturally knotted tightly together. When the bag was made, the polymers were stretched out flat. Heating the empty bag up releases the polymers so they can scrunch up again.

SOLAR STILL

YOU WILL NEED:
★ A sunny day!
★ A large bowl
★ A small jar or glass
★ Plastic wrap
★ A pitcher of water
★ Salt
★ A tablespoon
★ Small, clean stones or marbles

If you were ever stranded in the wilderness, this cool experiment could save your life by creating drinkable water from salt water!

Step 1

Put some salt in a pitcher of water. Add about 4 tablespoons of salt to 1 quart (1 liter) of water. Stir thoroughly.

Step 2

Pour enough salty water into a large bowl so that it is about 2 inches (5 cm) deep.

Step 3

Place the small jar or glass in the center of the bowl of water. Make sure the top of the jar is above the salt water, but well below the top of the large bowl. You'll probably need to put some small stones or marbles in the glass to weigh it down and stop it floating in the water.

Step 4

Stretch some plastic wrap over the top of the large bowl and make an airtight seal.

Step 5

Place a marble in the center of the plastic wrap, directly over the jar to make the plastic slope down into the middle.

Step 6

Put your solar still outside in the sun. Leave it for at least 4 hours. The longer you leave it out, the more water you'll collect.

This experiment is marble-lous!

Step 7

When you are ready to check your solar still, take off the plastic wrap and look at the water that's collected in the jar. Do you think it's salty or fresh? Taste it and see!

HOW DOES IT WORK?

The heat from the sun causes water to evaporate from the bowl, leaving the salt behind. As this happens, the water vapor hits the plastic wrap and condenses back into liquid water again. The marble weighing the plastic down makes the water run down into the jar, thereby allowing you to collect fresh water!

FEELING HOT AND COLD

YOU WILL NEED:

* ★ 2 small containers e.g. plastic buckets
* ★ A large bowl
* ★ Hot water
* ★ Cold water and ice cubes
* ★ Room temperature water
* ★ A towel

Why is it that people feel temperature differently? When some people are snuggled in coats, other people are walking around in T-shirts. This experiment tests how this is possible.

Step 1

Pour cold water and ice cubes into a bucket.

Step 2

Pour hot (not boiling) water into another bucket.

Step 3

Fill a large bowl with water at room temperature.

Step 4

Put one hand in the hot water and the other hand in the cold water. Your hands should stay in the water for a few minutes.

Step 5

Take both hands out of the buckets, and plunge them into the large bowl. The hand from the cold bucket will feel warm, and the hand from the warm bucket will feel cold!

HOW DOES IT WORK?

This experiment shows that the way we feel temperature is relative. If you have just been in a warm place, room temperature might feel quite cool, but if you have been in a cold place, room temperature will feel lovely and warm.

The hot water should not to be TOO hot—don't burn yourself!

Step 6

Take your hands out of the water and dry them.

ICE CREAM IN A BAG

YOU WILL NEED:

★ 1/2 cup whole milk or cream

★ Sugar and salt

★ Vanilla flavoring

★ 2 small, sealable freezer bags

★ 1 large, sealable freezer bag

★ 4 cups of ice cubes

★ A rolling pin

★ A clean dish towel

★ Woolly gloves

Here is a simple way to make ice cream in just ten minutes—you'll never chase after the ice cream truck again!

Finally! An experiment that's good to eat!

Step 1

Pour ½ cup whole milk or cream, 1 tablespoon of sugar, and ½ teaspoon of vanilla flavoring into a small sealable freezer bag.

Step 2

Push out as much air as possible as you seal the bag.

16

Step 3

Place the first bag inside the second small bag, squeezing out the air.

Step 4

Seal the second bag.

Watch your fingers! And be careful with the table too!

Step 5

Make some crushed ice. Fold the ice cubes in a clean towel and beat them with a wooden rolling pin on a hard surface.

Step 6

Put the crushed ice in the large freezer bag and add a tablespoon of salt.

Step 7

Put the smaller bags into the middle of the crushed ice and salt mixture in the large freezer bag. Squeeze out as much air as possible and then seal the bag.

Time to get the woolly gloves on!

Step 8

Wearing the gloves, shake and squish the bag so that the ice surrounds the mixture. It should take 5 to 10 minutes for the mixture to become ice cream!

Mmmm. Yummy!

HOW DOES IT WORK?

The salt lowers the freezing point of the ice. This means it melts faster. When it melts, it takes in energy in the form of heat from the surrounding environment—in this case, the ice cream mixture, which cools it down until it freezes.

SOLAR OVEN

Harness the power of the Sun to make tasty treats for you and your friends!

YOU WILL NEED:

- ★ An empty pizza box
- ★ Black water-based paint
- ★ A paint brush
- ★ A black polyethylene bag
- ★ Aluminum foil
- ★ Plastic wrap
- ★ A glue stick, tape, scissors, and a ruler
- ★ A marker pen
- ★ Marshmallows, chocolate, and cookies
- ★ A paper plate
- ★ A wooden stick
- ★ A warm, sunny day!

Step 1

Paint the bottom and the sides of the outside of the pizza box black. Allow the paint to dry.

Step 2

Draw a 1 inch (25 mm) border on the front and sides of the top of the pizza box. Cut along the line with scissors.

Step 3

Open the flap in the lid of the box. Stick a square of aluminum foil on the inside of the flap with the glue stick.

Step 4

Seal the opening made by the flap with a piece of plastic wrap.

Step 5

Line the inside of the pizza box with a folded black polyethylene bag. Tape it to the sides to keep it in place.

Step 6

Find a sunny spot in the yard. Close the window in the pizza box and prop open the flap with a stick. Adjust the box so that the foil reflects the maximum sunlight through the window into the oven.

Step 7

Your oven is ready—let's make s'mores! Put a cookie on a paper plate and cover with marshmallows and chocolate.

My taste circuits are tingling!

Step 8

Check on progress in the oven every 10 minutes. Make sure sunlight is still reflected into the oven. On a nice, sunny day, it should take about 30 minutes.

HOW DOES IT WORK?

The idea of a solar oven is to capture as much of the Sun's heat as possible. The color black absorbs heat, so this makes sure that the cooking area of the box soaks up as much warmth as possible. Silver reflects heat, so the lid is used to gather more of the sun's heat and direct it to the food. The plastic wrap acts like glass in a greenhouse, allowing the light and heat in, but not letting it out again. All three together make a pretty good oven!

SOAP SCULPTURES

Create your own fun soap sculptures just using the microwave!

Step 1

Put a bar of soap on a paper plate. Ask an adult to put it in the microwave on a high setting for 1 minute.

Step 2

Watch through the closed door of the microwave. The soap should expand and grow!

Oooh, microwaves. My favorite kind of radiation!

Step 3

After one minute, the soap should have expanded, but if the original bar shape is still visible, microwave it for another 30 seconds.

Flatten the bottom of the sculpture so it stands on the plinth.

Step 4

Allow several minutes for the soap to cool before you touch it. Remove it from the microwave with an oven mitt.

Light your finished sculptures in a dramatic way with a desk lamp and take photographs of them!

Step 5

Repeat the process for each sculpture you want to make. Get your friends to make some and see who can get the best results! Make some plinths from aerosol can tops to show off your work.

HOW DOES IT WORK?

When the microwave is turned on, the water molecules in the soap are heated up and turn to vapor. The vapor forms bubbles which expand in the heat, making the soap expand in weird and wonderful ways!

THE JUMPING COIN TRICK

Amaze your family and friends by making a coin jump into the air without touching it!

★ A glass bottle with a narrow neck, such as a wine bottle

★ A coin—the right size to fit on the mouth of the bottle

★ Hot water

★ Ice cubes

★ 2 bowls—big enough for the bottle to stand in

Step 1

Put an empty bottle without a lid in a bowl and pack ice cubes around it. Allow it to cool for a few minutes. While you are waiting, ask an adult to pour some hot water into a bowl for you.

This is the lazy way to toss a coin.

Step 2

Take the bottle out of the bowl. Put a coin on the mouth of the bottle.

Step 3

Carefully lift the bottle and lower it into the bowl of hot water.

Wow! It's like magic!

Step 4

After a little while, the coin will jump off the bottle!

HOW DOES IT WORK?

As the bottle is heated, so is the air inside it. As the air warms up, it starts to expand, pushing on the coin and making it jump.

BALLOON FLAME

YOU WILL NEED:

* ★ Balloons
* ★ A candle on a saucer
* ★ Matches
* ★ Safety glasses or sunglasses
* ★ Water

You (and your adult helper) will need nerves of steel to test this fiery experiment!

Get ready to cover your ears!

Step 1

Blow up a balloon and tie a knot in the end.

Step 2

Light a candle and then put on your safety glasses or sunglasses.

Step 3

Hold the balloon in the flame! What happens?

Step 4

Add some water to another balloon, then blow it up and knot it.

Step 5

Put the part of the balloon holding the water into the flame.

Step 6

Remove the balloon from the flame and examine it!

HOW DOES IT WORK?

This is all about the conduction of heat energy. When the balloon is full of air, the candle flame melts the balloon's surface, so it explodes. That's because the heat remained concentrated over the candle. Water conducts heat better than air, so it can absorb some of the heat—keeping the balloon from melting.

JAR WARS

"Insulators" are materials that stop heat energy spreading. They are used to keep things warm or cold. This experiment is a hunt for the best insulators.

YOU WILL NEED:

★ 3 clean jars with lids, similar in size and shape

★ A clean sock

★ Bubble wrap

★ An old newspaper

★ Ice-cold water

★ A clock, watch, or timer

★ A cooking thermometer

★ Tape

★ Scissors

This certainly is the "coolest" experiment!

Step 1

Check that your jars are clean and that they have lids that fit well.

Step 2

Wrap each jar in a different material, with only one layer of material covering the sides of the jar.

Step 3

Secure the materials with tape but don't cover the tops of the jars. Stand the jars in a row.

Step 4

Fill all the jars with ice-cold water.

Step 5

Record the temperature of the water in each jar. Put all the lids on the water-filled jars. Note the time.

Step 6

Wait five minutes—check the time. Take the temperature again in each jar. Compare the temperatures. Which jar kept the water coldest?

HOW DOES IT WORK?

Materials that are not good at passing on heat are called insulators. If the heat isn't passed on from the air to the water in our experiment, the water will remain cold for longer.

GLOSSARY

absorb (ub-SORB) To suck up or take in.

condense (kun-DENTS) To cool and change from a gas to a liquid.

conduction (kun-DUK-shun) The transfer of heat energy through a material.

density (DEN-seh-tee) The amount of a substance that can fit within a particular space.

evaporate (ih-VA-puh-rayt) To change from a liquid state to a state of gas because of increased heat.

insulator (INT-suh-lay-tur) A substance that slows or blocks the transfer of energy, such as heat energy.

molecule (MAH-lih-kyool) A group of atoms bonded together to form a chemical compound. It is the smallest particle that still has all the chemical properties of a substance.

polymer (PAH-luh-mer) A chemical structure made up of repeating chains of molecules.

radiation (ray-dee-AY-shun) The process of sending out energy.

reflect (rih-FLEKT) To prevent the passage of something, causing it to change direction.

solar (SOH-ler) Having to do with the Sun.

still (STIL) A piece of equipment that uses boiling and cooling to separate the ingredients that are combined in a liquid.

water vapor (WAH-ter VAY-pur) Water that is in the form of a gas.

Searching glossary database...

FURTHER READING

Cassino, Mark, and Jon Nelson. *The Story of Snow: The Science of Winter's Wonder*. San Francisco: Chronicle Books, 2009.

Gardner, Robert. *Sizzling Science Projects With Heat and Energy*. Berkeley Heights, NJ: Enslow Elementary Books, 2006.

Guillain, Charlotte. *Hot or Cold.* Properties of Materials. Chicago: Heinemann-Raintree, 2010.

Latta, Sara L. *Ice Scientist: Careers in the Frozen Antarctic*. Berkeley Heights, NJ: Enslow Publishers, 2009.

Moore, Rob. *Why Does Water Evaporate?: All About Heat and Temperature*. New York: PowerKids Press, 2010.

Murphy, Pat, and the Exploratorium. *Exploratopia: More Than 400 Kid-Friendly Experiments and Explorations for Curious Minds*. New York: Little, Brown Books, 2006.

Simon, Seymour. *Global Warming*. New York: Collins Publishing, 2010.

TIME for Kids. *TIME for Kids Super Science Book*. New York: TIME for Kids Books, 2009.

Websites

For web resources related to the subject of this book, go to: www.windmillbooks.com/weblinks and select this book's title.

INDEX

These experiments are just a warm-up.

Don't get cold feet!